Monsters
We Make
Stories From The Edge Of Sanity

Brando Calzada

DEDICATION

To my wife and my daughter —

You are the love that saved me.

You are the reason the demons inside me learned to quiet down, the reason the man I fought so hard to become finally had something worth fighting for.

Your love gave me peace I didn't know existed.

Your presence taught me that monsters can be tamed, and broken men can still build something beautiful.

Everything I am now, everything I will ever be, begins with you.

And to my Brother and sisters

The ones still wrestling with their own shadows, their own history, their own ghosts.

I know your battles.

I've seen your pain.

I love you more than I ever learned to say.

This book is a reminder that none of us were born lost —

we were shaped by things we didn't choose

AND SURVIVED THINGS MOST WON'T EVER UNDERSTAND.

IF YOU'RE STILL FIGHTING, KEEP GOING.

IF YOU EVER FEEL ALONE, YOU'RE NOT.

AND IF YOU EVER FORGET WHO YOU ARE, REMEMBER THIS:

WE COME FROM THE SAME STORM,

BUT NONE OF US HAVE TO DROWNED IN IT.

BRENDA

NIDIAN

ALINA

LLARELI

JUAN

Acknowledgement

To the men I met inside prisons, rehabs, and the darkest corners of the world:

You shaped my understanding of trauma, pain, madness, and survival.

Your stories—loud or quiet, broken or brave—helped me see the humanity behind the labels society throws at us. This book carries pieces of all of you.

To those who work in mental health, therapy, and addiction recovery:

Your work saves lives that don't always know how to ask for saving.

Thank you for giving people like me the tools our childhoods never provided.

And finally, to anyone who has ever wrestled with their own monsters:

This book is for you.

Not to justify anything we've done or survived, but to remind you that you are not alone.

Healing is not clean, and redemption is not guaranteed—but it's possible.

If my story becomes a small light in your fight, then every wound that built this book was worth it.

CONTENTS

Introduction

In search of my true identity, I have listened to many audiobooks and read countless books to understand my own mind. I have started several college majors without finishing, and launched businesses that ended in failure. I have held many jobs—some important and some not, but these two I will write about explained why they marked me and made me understand myself but also made me question my sanity. Anyway, I could never keep one for long. I always kept some employment to stay afloat but also started side hustles, from construction to selling drugs for the cartel, driven by the same goal of becoming financially free, and the dream of owning my plane.

For a time I thought I was addicted to the adrenaline of getting away with things. Over time I realised I was actually chasing the excitement of meeting small goals. Researchers note that sensation-seeking behaviour is not driven by adrenaline alone; dopamine and serotonin systems also influence impulsivity and risk-taking, and dysregulation in these systems can lead to craving states similar to substance use disorders. Looking back, I see that living in chaos felt like peace. I constantly needed a new challenge, a fresh thrill. Studies suggest that some people may unconsciously create drama and crises in their lives to trigger the body's stress response and relieve negative moods, which resonates with my pattern of constant upheaval.

Growing up in a Hispanic household, therapy wasn't an option — it was an insult. Men were taught to be silent, to "aguántate," to survive without breaking, crying, or questioning. According to research from the American Psychological Association, Latino men are statistically among the least likely demographic to seek mental health treatment, not because they don't need it, but because culturally they are conditioned to believe asking for help equals weakness. Boys are told "Los hombres no lloran," and emotional expression becomes shame. Instead of communication, we inherit silence. Instead of treatment, we develop coping mechanisms disguised as personality.

So like many men raised in trauma, I self-medicated. I didn't call it depression or anxiety back then — I called it normal. At eighteen I began drinking heavily, not to party or celebrate, but to numb thoughts my culture told me I wasn't allowed to speak out loud. Alcohol became the only therapist I believed I deserved. Research shows that children exposed to prolonged violence and emotional neglect often develop neurobiological patterns similar to combat PTSD — hyper-vigilance, emotional detachment, stored rage, and difficulty regulating fear and anger. Studies from Harvard and Yale show that trauma during childhood reshapes the brain's stress response, creating a nervous system always prepared for danger — even when danger isn't there. For years, alcohol was my only form of treatment. I used it to escape my racing mind, my childhood echoes, my nightmares. I didn't get real help until I was thirty-three.

At home, there was love and violence mixed together. My father wasn't really around when we were growing up, he worked in California while we lived in Mexico, but the time I would spend with him during his visits we're my favorite, he was gentle, he was caring, he was loving, and he loved and taught me the beautiful side of fatherhood. He taught me how to work the land, how to tame mustangs, how to be a man of good even with all his generational traumas. He went to college and succeeded to finish a psychology major. He was firm but caring, but could never stop being a womanizer that finally broke our family. (I love you Dad.)

There were six of us, and our parents divorced in 2000 when I was ten. There was no structure or stable role model in my life, only a lot of freedom. My mother carried her own generational trauma—poverty, migration, betrayal, abandonment—and she passed that pain down the only way she knew: through mental, physical and emotional abuse. I grew up believing her word: that I was stupid, an idiot, someone who was dumb and couldn't stay still.

When she was overwhelmed, she beat me violently. I still remember the sting of cables, belts and open hands, the way she would keep swinging long after the lesson was learned, the way my body would bruise and bleed and my mind would disconnect. Some days I felt like a punching bag; other days like a burden she couldn't afford to have. I

learned early that love could turn into rage in a second, that safety didn't exist, that the person who was supposed to feed, love and protect you could also be the one who hurt you.

Now that I am older, I see her differently. I understand she was also a product of generational trauma, survival mode, and a culture that told her this was discipline. She was a wounded woman trying to raise children while fighting her own invisible wars. I have forgiven her—not because what she did was right, but because holding on to that anger was killing me from the inside.our relationship has changed since Michael appeared in her life and thought her love, respect and true Affection.

Around us, the men in my family were not examples of stability either. Most of my uncles and surrounding family members were ex-convicts, drug dealers, womanisers. Prison stories and cartel business were spoken about like weather and football: casual, normal, part of daily life. I grew up thinking this was what being a man looked like—hustling, cheating, doing time, coming back home and starting over.

Later, standing in a coroner's transport room cutting and burning bodies for science, I caught myself wondering: if I am dismembering and cremating people to the sound of music, how different am I really from a psychopath or that person I try so hard to avoid becoming, or even my uncles, who do the same in the name of money or revenge? Where is the line between "necessary work" and brutality? Between "justice" and violence? Those questions haunt every chapter of this book.

With no stable father figure and no safe emotional space, I gravitated toward the wrong people. By twelve I was stealing car stereos; by thirteen I was selling marijuana in high school. That same year I stabbed someone in the face and was kicked out of Colorado. My father decided returning to California was a bad idea, so he sent me to Mexico, where I met cartel members—some of whom still work, while others are dead or missing.

Being around them made me realise I could never behead someone or saw off hands for stealing food for their children. I couldn't torture a person while listening to cumbia. I couldn't stay on drugs without feeling guilty, dirty or miserable. My conscience wouldn't let me become the next Pablo Escobar. Studies have found that childhood maltreatment can disrupt the development of self-care, leading children to neglect their own feelings and self-worth; later this can predispose them to risky behaviours like drug abuse. Trauma has also been linked to structural changes in brain regions such as the anterior cingulate cortex, prefrontal cortex, corpus callosum and hippocampus, along with increased amygdala reactivity and reduced striatal response to reward. I didn't know the science then, but I sensed something was wrong in my mind, even if my heart meant well.

After quitting drugs and dealing, I looked for jobs that would help me understand who I was. I even studied criminal justice with a focus on forensic science at the Community College of Aurora. I have been on both sides of the law: I have worked in correctional settings and been incarcerated. To this day I am still searching my soul and trying to understand myself by examining the mistakes others have made. Many of my adult character traits came from watching others fail.

As a child I dreamed of becoming an astronaut. Growing up in a small town with small minds, that dream felt too big to share,so I said wanted to be a pilot. Every morning my uncle Juan Cosme the only person I felt believed and the only person I shared this goal with, would stop me on my way to school and ask what I wanted to be. I always said "a pilot," and he would ask if I would give him a ride when I learned. I always said yes. He smiled, gave me a candy, and sent me to school. Unfortunately life didn't let him ride with me—or I took too long to learn to fly. Even then I had a drive to improve my financial situation.

At age four, after being born and raised in California, my father moved us to Guerrero, Mexico, so he could legalize my mother's and sister's status in the United States. I don't remember the move, but I recall thinking that if all the people from our Californian neighbourhood had left this place, it must be hell.

Most of my major memories began in Mexico, except for the deaths, overdoses and violence I saw in California at a young age. When we moved to Mexico, my classroom had no windows or doors—just a chalkboard, old student chairs and many kids with no shoes. I couldn't comprehend such a stark difference from California schools. Two completely different worlds.

The bell rang for lunch, the only familiar sound. My mother sometimes brought food, but when she was busy she gave us money to buy lunch. I noticed many of my new friends didn't eat. I shared my lunch and made friends quickly. Then my entrepreneurial mind started working.

My first business, if it can be called that, was selling pencils at school. I saw the demand and began selling pencils my father brought from California. Soon I even stole pencils from classmates to create scarcity and undercut the woman who sold supplies at the gate by offering a 50% discount. Within a month she was no longer my competition. Things were going well: I bought fancy supplies, good food to share with friends, and even a Coke now and then, forbidden at home.

Unfortunately it didn't last. My little business stopped abruptly when my mother discovered I'd taken the pencils my father bought for us.

My sister had noticed everyone had the same pencil. One day, after feeding my father's cattle, she warned me to wear two shirts because my mother was about to beat me. After bleeding from my legs and back for three days, I saved about 300 pesos and felt both accomplished and free. I immediately looked for my next move—something that didn't involve another beating.

Not long after, I saw a man in a brand-new truck followed by three more trucks driven by bodyguards. Everyone knew him except me; they called him Chalino Estrada. I asked my mother what he did. "He's a criminal," she said. It was the first successful drug dealer I had seen. The town was miserably poor but happy. I told my mother I wanted to be a criminal when I grew up. "You don't know what you're saying," she replied. To me he looked like a cowboy or a farmer. I wanted his boots, and his trucks but also his gun and respect or fear towards him. My dream of owning a plane still lingered.

To get there, I launched another venture. My father had about ten cows and a few horses. My mother allowed neighbours to pasture their donkeys on our land because of a natural spring and green pastures. One day, as I fed the animals, the neighbours' kids were picking up manure. They told me the local brick plant paid twenty pesos per sack. I started collecting manure too. It wasn't 2.50 pesos per pencil; it was twenty per sack. My mother gave me sacks of grain for the cows and I filled them with manure after school. I offered to clean neighbours' lots and made around 500 pesos a week—a huge achievement for a six-year-old in rural Mexico.

With the 300 pesos I made from selling pencils, I bought more sacks. But when my mother found my stash of 2,500 pesos, she demanded to know where it came from. I explained my business plan, bracing for a beating. She was surprised and impressed, and decided to have my sisters collect manure too. Suddenly it was embarrassing to see my siblings doing it. I slowly quit.

By 2000 it was time to return to California. I was nine. There I saw crime, murder and overdoses. Shootings were a daily norm. My father moved us to Denver, Colorado, to scape this life.. Soon my parents' differences exploded; they divorced in the worst way—violence, screaming, drinking and insults. It hit us hard.

I tried to be strong but cried in the bathroom for hours, sometimes turning on the water so no one would hear. My mother met another man who showed her love appreciation and respect . I hadn't really known my father; he worked long hours to provide for six kids. I was the oldest male and had long hair. After my mother left, I cut my hair and went completely rebellious. I realised I had to adopt my mother's fierceness to protect my sisters and myself. At one point she had fist-fought men to defend my teenage sisters from lewd comments. Now she was gone.

In high school I was given a corner to sell marijuana. As I sank deeper into gang life, my responsibilities grew. One was to look after the girlfriend of a major distributor. She was a senior and six months pregnant; I was a freshman. One day after lunch, as I walked her to class, three rival gang members and a slender boy approached us. One punched her in the stomach. The others punched me.

I pulled a metal pen from my back pocket and stabbed them. Blood splattered. Two ran. The one I focused on lay on the floor. I kept stabbing his face, wondering why I couldn't stop my rage.Security grabbed me. He didn't press charges. I was suspended for two weeks. The judge ordered me out of Colorado, wanting me back in California.

When the two weeks ended, I returned to my corner. A van pulled up and opened fire. I ran. I had never been shot at. My sister and I fled to my cousin's house, where my mother picked us up. Everyone at school knew about the shooting. My parents reunited briefly to decide what to do. My father refused to send me back to California, so they sent me to Mexico again.

Back in Mexico, the freedom pushed me further astray. I drank and used drugs. One day, after smoking marijuana, I tossed the roach. Days later a plant sprouted—a sign. I began growing weed; soon my backyard was full of plants. Money flowed, but like my other ventures, it didn't last. The cartels moved in. It was 2004; cartels were unheard of in that region until then. A cousin and I quit drugs and drinking and took up boxing that didn't worked either, soon after my cousin joined the cartel and lost his right eye after a murder attempt,. I felt lonely; money, freedom and respect weren't worth it.

My father and I decided I should return. By 2006 I was sixteen . I was a junior in high school when I met the mother of my son. I became a father. I tattooed my last name on my neck,it was said that when the Carter would cut you in to pieces, many only recognized the bodies by the tattoos,I had accepted my faith at only fourteen, back in Colorado that same tattoo hold me back from many many good opportunities, having survived many traumatic events. I was reckless and wild, and my options were limited. But I hadn't forgotten my dream of owning a plane; the boots I once wanted were forgotten,by now my goals had grew.

By then I'd sold drugs, stolen car stereos and anything else I could. With a son to care for,and force to marry at 17, I redirected my life. I finished high school at twenty-three and enrolled in college. My first marriage failed after eight years. I was devastated but kept going. Most of my family in Colorado was in law enforcement, so I chose that path. I knew what a criminal was; I had been one. I wanted to be on the other side.

I majored in criminal justice and excelled in crime scene investigation. Inspired by Detective Joe Kenda, I took security jobs. After completing the class, my professor—who had attended the Aurora theater shooting—asked if I could handle being around dead bodies. I thought I could. I was wrong.

I had seen death before. The first dead body I saw was in California when I was four. A young man in our apartment complex overdosed;

14

I remember his hand hanging outside the sheet as he was carried away. Working in a hospital later, I bagged and wheeled bodies to the morgue. When my stepfather died in that same hospital, the place changed forever.

I thought I could handle the coroner job, but nothing prepared me for it. The building looked like a normal house in an industrial area, with black smoke rising from what looked like a chimney. An older man had me sign paperwork. Other employees arrived: a 350-pound white man with glasses, another large man with glasses, a rockabilly-looking guy in his fifties with a pompadour and chain wallet, and me, a five-foot-seven Mexican with tattoos up to my neck, all of us in suits like all going to court.

The manager asked us to unload a van with twenty-five bodies donated to science. The boxes went into a walk-in fridge; when it was full we stacked them on racks outside. Many leaked. The smell was awful—more like a meat market than death. At one point I picked up a small box, thinking it was a child. It wasn't. It was filled with organs. The box opened, and a heart and liver landed on my new shoes. I grimaced under my mask.

The other workers finished unloading while I cleaned myself. We dismembered bodies to remove pacemakers. Some had no heads, brains or limbs, depending on what medical students needed. I opened the giant oven every hour to check on the bodies. As they burned, their feet and hands would twitch because the nerves were burning; I didn't know that. I separated ashes from metal and pulverised the remaining bones in a giant blender.

My first call with the rockabilly coworker was to pick up a 98-year-old veteran with an amputated foot who died watching Westerns. The bed couldn't fit in his narrow hallway, so I carried him. He had been dead for hours; the smell of decay pressed against my face, vaporub became my best friend. We dropped him at a funeral home.

I needed to pee, but the bathroom was down a dark hallway lined with bodies waiting for makeup. I decided to wait. Back in the van, my partner received another call: a man had hanged himself in his closet. Police had ruled it a suicide. The apartment had no elevator; the July heat was stifling. The stench of alcohol and death was overwhelming.

We cut the belt, and the body fell stiffly. We bagged him and carried him down three flights. The smell was so close to my face it still haunts me. People watched from their doorways as we loaded him into the van. Next we went to the Jefferson County coroner's office. A 65-year-old sergeant opened the garage. He wheeled out a 45-year-old woman who had been stabbed seven times by her lover. Her autopsy table was still covered in fresh blood. She had a long cut from shoulder to pelvis.

We slid a bag under her, banded her wrist, tagged her toe and zipped her up. We dropped those bodies because the van only held two. Then we drove to a warehouse to weigh them and tag the bags pink or blue depending on their sex. The big fridge smelled like death. Some bodies were unbagged; others were John or Jane Does. Three huge ovens burned bodies all day.

A pony-tailed Hispanic man no taller than five-foot-four listened to Pantera while feeding bodies into the flames. I stepped outside to breathe. The reality of death hit me like a panic attack. I thought of my family—my parents, siblings, wife and daughter—and wanted to run and scream. I called my wife. "I don't think I can do this," I said. She told me to finish the shift and quit. I felt calmer after hearing her voice. I put my mask back on and went back to work.

We went to a gas station to buy snacks. My partner got Doritos and a slurpee. I couldn't eat, my stomach was revolting, We got a call from the hospital: an older, heavyset woman who had donated her body to science. Then a call from a donor place that harvested eyes.

We drove far out of town to a facility where students studied bodies and cremated them. Inside, the smell of bleach was stronger than decay. Stainless steel sinks lined the walls. Knives and saws hung above them. Six clean autopsy tables stood in the middle. Five huge ovens loomed to the left. Straight ahead, illuminated by the open garage door, was a shiny metal walk in fridge.

My partner said I didn't have to go in, but my curiosity pushed me. He set his Doritos on a corpse's chest and filled out paperwork. I thought it was disrespectful, but he seemed used to it. He handed me keys. I opened the fridge door. Inside were shelves of body parts. Legs on one side, torsos on another, arms and hands on another, heads on another, and full bodies in front.

It was the worst place I had ever seen. I thought of my stepfather, who had donated his body to science. I wondered if someone had treated him like this. I wanted to cry. On the drive back, I sat silently and watched the sun go down. My mind was full of questions. Where is the line between medical students cutting up bodies and cartel members dismembering them? How do we accept such work? Are we any different when we listen to music while burning bodies?

I called the manager after my shift and told him I appreciated the opportunity but I wasn't the right person for the job. He answered he understood and that he appreciated the call,after 6 pm I headed to the hospital. My father-in-law and brother-in-law worked there; they asked how it went. I said, "Horrible." Right then I decided to quit crime scene investigation, although my hyperactive mind kept asking questions.

My next job was at a forensic mental health facility. I can't reveal names, and I didn't verify all the stories residents told me beyond their criminal and medical records. Their diagnoses ranged from ADHD to schizophrenia, borderline personality disorder, hallucinations and dissociative identity disorder.

I decided to listen to their stories and write this book. I knew I would only get answers from people who were truly sick—those who had committed murder, rape, necrophilia, zoophilia and, worst of all, pedophilia. Unfortunately I left with more questions. Everything in this book is their reality and, in many ways, mine.

There was a women's section and a men's section. Each staff member was assigned three residents and was responsible for their medications, finances and daily needs. Residents were allowed to leave for medical appointments or therapy with permission. Before I started, I was down on my luck. My sister sent me the job listing to help. I applied and got the job quickly.

The first weeks were training—how to deal with these individuals, for the first time I realized mental health was real. Once assigned, each new employee received a white folder. Based on our demeanour , three residents were assigned. The folder listed medications, food restrictions, clothing sizes and special requirements. It also included a brief description of their crimes, criminal records and mental diagnoses.

We needed to understand who we were working with and how we could help them function outside if they were ever released. I started asking them about their past. Some were eager to talk; others were reserved. Over time all three of my residents shared their stories—some during smoke breaks, some at lunch, others during snowstorms. I wanted to understand their reality and what was going on in their heads.

This book tells their stories and mine

EL AMIGO

CHAPTER 1

Angel was what you'd call a Chicano. He grew up in Pueblo, Colorado, spoke broken Spanish except for the bad words, and had been diagnosed with bipolar disorder and hallucinations. His criminal file was thick. He'd been convicted of murder and rape. That's why I met him in a mental hospital instead of a regular prison.

I'm starting with his story because he was the first one who really opened up to me. We talked on the long one-hour smoke breaks. Over the course of months and seasons, with him pacing in circles and me sitting on the same bench, I wrote down what he told me.

This is how Angel said his life went.

The Journey to Mexico

In 1982, Angel got a letter from his mother. His grandmother Felix—his Nana—was very sick back in Chihuahua, Mexico. Doctors said she might not make it.

He'd visited Chihuahua as a kid, but it never felt like home. Pueblo was where he'd learned to fight, to hustle, to survive. Still, he decided to go see Nana before she died. He had one way to get there: a beat-up 1975 Japanese SX650 motorcycle he'd pieced together from junkyard parts in New Mexico.

He packed a small bag, a blanket, some tools, and kicked the bike to life. The desert roads heading south were long and empty. Hot air slapped his face. The vibration numbed his hands as the patched-up motor screamed along the dirt and broken asphalt. Mosquitos and dust stuck to his long hair. The air smelled like sage, gasoline and heat.

He hadn't seen his parents in years. The thought of Nana lying somewhere in an adobe house, breathing hard and fading, pulled him south. The thought of easy money dragged along right beside it. His motorcycle club in Pueblo had given him a list: marijuana, peyote, mushrooms, pills—things they believed were cheaper and stronger in Mexico. He figured he could bring enough back to buy himself a proper bike and maybe start over.

His father always talked about Nana as a curandera—a healer. She was the kind of woman people visited when doctors gave up: for cancers, diabetes, nervous attacks, curses. He used to say she could fly, that she talked to spirits, that she had saints and old gods mixed together on the same altar. Angel was seventeen and skeptical, like most kids.

"If she can cure everything," he'd argue, "how come she can't cure herself?"

Still, the stories stuck.

Hours later, his fuel ran low. He stopped at a tiny grocery in the middle of nowhere. No houses visible, only burros, cows and skinny dogs in the distance. Inside, the wooden floor creaked under his boots. A humming refrigerator buzzed in the corner. He grabbed a cold beer, then another, then a third.

"¿Sabes que tienes que pagar por esas cervezas?"

The voice behind him made him jump. He dropped the bottle; foam hissed across the floor.

He turned and froze. A girl his age—or a little older—stood there, beautiful in that dusty, simple way only small-town girls have. Dark hair, serious green eyes that didn't look away. He forgot how to speak.

She handed him a rag. "Clean it up," she ordered.

In broken Spanish he explained he was from Pueblo, Colorado, on his way to visit his sick grandmother Felix.

"¿La curandera?" she asked.

When he nodded, her face softened. She told him Nana's house was nine miles down the road. "Pay me for the gas and beer next time," she said, waving off his money. "Just hurry. Your grandma doesn't have much time."

Angel filled his tank and rode on, thinking more about the girl than the debt.

He knew he'd arrived when he saw his father's pickup in front of an adobe house with a straw roof. His mother was at the outdoor concrete sink, washing clothes with a bar of soap. He hugged her and kissed her forehead.

"Pásale, mijo," she said quietly. "Your presence will cheer your dad. Nana está muy mal."

Inside, the house was dim and cool. His father sat in a bamboo chair, hands planted on his knees, staring at the dirt floor. He wasn't crying, but his silence was heavy. Nana lay on a bamboo bed, shrunk down to almost nothing, eyes half-closed, breathing shallow.

Angel sat beside his father and just watched her chest rise and fall.

That night he slept outside in a hammock strung between two trees. The sky was so clear it didn't seem real. Stars burned like cold fire. The air turned chilly, but his poncho kept him warm. Around him he heard crickets, distant dogs, owls, donkeys, and a wolf far off.

In the dark, images of the store girl came back: her eyes, the way her hands didn't shake when she spoke to him, how she'd just trusted him to come back and pay. With his broken Spanish, he tried to think of what he would say if he saw her again

At dawn his mother woke him gently. After a quick breakfast under a shade made of dried hay, his father saddled a one-eyed mule and motioned for Angel to climb on. Neither said much.

They rode for hours. The mule's rough gait turned Angel's legs numb. The desert stretched out, then slowly gave way to small green valleys and thin rivers, then back to dry ground. Finally they stopped in what looked like the middle of nowhere.

Angel looked around. "Why here?"

His father tied the mule to a scrubby tree, walked a few yards, and grabbed what looked like a tree stump. He heaved it aside, revealing a square hole in the ground, about three feet across. Cool air rose up from the darkness.

His father climbed down first. "Sígueme, nomás escucha mi voz," he called.

Angel lowered himself into the hole. The light dimmed. His hands slid along damp rock. As his eyes adjusted, he saw thin beams of sunlight filtering through cracks above. The air changed—turned cooler, wetter, quiet in a way that made his own breathing sound loud.

His father told him this cave had formed when a meteorite hit sideways long ago, carving a tunnel and a chamber underground. Locals called it el valle de los dioses—the valley of the gods.

Inside, the world felt different. Dripping water echoed softly. The ceiling hung with stalactites that shone when the light hit them. An underground pool reflected the faint glow. Pale ferns and moss grew where no sun should reach. Mushrooms clustered along a fallen slab of rock.

Angel couldn't believe it was real. It felt like stepping into one of his father's stories.

"This is where your Nana and other curanderos come for plants," his father said. "Some of these don't grow anywhere else. And listen to me, cabrón—don't eat mushrooms que no conoces. Los hongos son espíritu. Some help you. Some ruin you."

They sat on a flat rock. His father made a small fire, filled a pot with water from the pool and boiled it. He sliced a couple of mushrooms, dropped them in, and handed Angel a cup.

"First time is with me," he said. "Después tú decides."

The tea tasted bitter and earthy. After twenty minutes, Angel's stomach twisted. He vomited on the cave floor. His father just nodded.

Then the cave started to breathe. At least that's how Angel later described it. The air pulsed against his skin. Colors he'd never seen slid across the rock walls. He felt himself moving through spirals of light, like being pulled down a tunnel without his body.

A male figure appeared—half shadow, half light. The presence spoke without moving its lips, answering questions Angel hadn't asked out loud:

About good and evil.
 About reincarnation.
 About how humans are energy that recycles through different bodies.
 About one god living inside everyone, and the way our choices write our own lives.
 About other worlds beyond Earth.

It wasn't like hearing a voice; it was like remembering something he'd always known but forgotten.

When Angel woke, he was lying on the cave floor. His pants were wet; ants crawled on his legs, biting. His head hurt. The fire was out.

A faint line of light came from the entrance. His father was sitting nearby, smoking.

"They spoke to you," his father said quietly. "Está bien. Te aceptaron. You'll understand later."

A Week in the Sacred Cave

After that first trip, Angel thought he was done. But his father had other plans.

He told Angel he would stay in the cave for a week. No distractions. No noise. "You want answers?" his father said. "You need to listen without the world yelling."

Angel brought only a little food and water. The rest, he had to handle.

The first day, the darkness scared him. Without sunlight, time stopped making sense. He followed the cave wall with one hand, leaving small stones as markers so he wouldn't get lost. He found a narrow chamber where condensation ran in tiny streams down the rock. He made that his spot.

He listened. To the water. To his own heartbeat. To the echo of his breathing.

On the second night, he repeated what his father had shown him. He mixed mushrooms carefully, boiled them, and prayed over the cup. He built a small altar with stones, set a candle on it, and whispered simple prayers: for protection, for guidance, for forgiveness. He remembered stories of the "world tree," the axis that connects the underworld, earth and sky. He imagined a tree growing from the center of the cave straight up through the rock into the stars.

The mushrooms hit harder that night. He lay on the damp floor and felt himself sink through layers of earth. He saw colors, patterns, and heard songs that felt older than language.

Figures appeared—ancestors, or at least that's what he believed. Some welcomed him. Some looked stern. One spoke of the "four waters":

- Numbers and patterns—the language of mathematics
- Cosmic geometry—the shapes and movement of stars
- Music—to bring the soul back to balance
- Plants—to heal the body and open the mind

He understood that all of this was part of his inheritance, whether he wanted it or not.

By the fourth day he was hungry and angry. His small stash of food was almost gone. He chewed bitter roots he found near the entrance. He drank from the pool, careful not to fall in. He bathed once, teeth chattering as the cold water hit him.

Fear came in waves. Darkness magnified every doubt. At his worst moments, he scratched shallow cuts into his arm with a rock, just to remind himself he still had a body.

On the seventh day he crawled toward the exit. When he emerged, the sunlight stabbed his eyes. The world felt too bright, too loud, too fast.

His father was waiting with the mule, sitting quietly in the same spot where they'd descended. He didn't ask, "What did you see?" or "What did you learn?"

He just hugged his son and said, "Ya saliste. Eso es lo importante."

Angel didn't have language yet for what had changed, but he knew he wasn't the same kid who'd gone down

After the cave, life didn't turn magic or holy. It went back to being complicated and ugly, like it always was.

Angel went back to visiting the girl at the small store. Her name was Crystal. They fell into a simple rhythm: he'd help her stock shelves, carry sacks of feed, and in between they'd talk. Her Spanish ran circles around him, but somehow they understood each other. Eventually they developed a beautiful relationship.

One afternoon, the sky grew dark and it started to rain. Real rain—the kind that hits hard and straight. They laughed as they ran outside, letting the downpour wash the dust off their clothes. Angel slipped his arm around her waist; she leaned into him. For a minute, everything felt clean.

Then a truck roared past, spraying muddy water all over them. Corridos blared from the stereo. Two men stepped out—sons of a rich rancher who owned half the town. Everyone knew them. Everyone feared them. They acted like they owned the roads, the store, and anyone who worked in it.

They walked in without greeting anyone. Crystal's body stiffened. She wiped her face, took a breath, and went back inside to ring them up. When they came out, Angel saw something in her eyes he didn't like: forced calm, tension in her jaw.

"¿Qué te dijeron?" he asked.

"Son unos estúpidos," she said, brushing it off. But she didn't meet his eyes.

Soon after, he saw the younger brother waiting outside the store. As Angel approached, the man blocked the door.

"¿Qué haces aquí, pinche gabacho?" he sneered. Before Angel could answer, the rancher shoved him hard. Angel hit the dirt, palms scraping, teeth biting the inside of his cheek. He tasted blood and humiliation.

Memories of Crystal in the rain flashed through his mind. The cave. His father's talk of spirits and choice. Everything tangled into one hot knot of rage.

Angel's hand went to the knife in his boot. He got up fast and drove the blade into the man's neck. Warmth sprayed across his knuckles. The man's eyes went wide. Angel didn't stop until the body went limp.

Inside, the older brother had grabbed Crystal by the wrists, pulling her toward the back of the store. She was twisting away, eyes wide. Angel stormed in, the knife still in his hand, red smeared across the blade.

He plunged it into the man's back. The gun the rancher had tucked into his belt went off as he fell, shattering a jar behind them. Crystal screamed. Angel grabbed a piece of shelving and swung, again and again, until the man collapsed and stayed down.

The store smelled like blood and spilled beans. The only sound was Crystal's shaking breath.

She shoved a rag at Angel. "Límpiate," she whispered.

Her hands trembled as she wiped his face. Fear and gratitude mixed in her eyes. She jammed food, water and a few bills into a bag and pushed it into his arms.

"Te amo," she said quickly. "Pero vete. They'll close the road to the border. If they catch you, they'll kill you."

Angel kissed her once and ran.

Hiding and Crossing

He hid in the cave his father had shown him. For two weeks he barely stepped outside.

The cool air that had once felt sacred now felt like a cell. He slept on a flat rock covered with leaves and his blanket. He rationed the food Crystal had given him, then moved to cactus fruit and roots near the entrance. He drank from the same pool he'd once seen as holy.

He listened to the drip of water and the flutter of bats. Sometimes he thought he heard voices calling his name. Sometimes he heard nothing but his own heart pounding.

He replayed the killings again and again. The shove. The knife going in. The sound Crystal made when he pulled her away. He tried to convince himself he'd done the right thing, but doubt gnawed at him in the dark.

Eventually, hunger and fear pushed him out. He decided that if he was going back to Pueblo, he wasn't going back empty-handed. Near the cave, he harvested weed from a hidden patch, cut peyote buttons and collected mushrooms that glowed faintly in the shade. He packed them under his blanket, strapped everything to his back and rolled his motorcycle out before dawn.

By the time he saw the border crossing, his nerves were shredded. He lined up behind cars, sweat trickling down his spine despite the heat having dropped with the evening. The bag under his clothes felt like it weighed a hundred pounds.

When his turn came, he forced his face into something calm. The officer asked where he was headed.

"Pueblo. A ver a mi abuela," he said.

The man studied him for what felt like a year, then waved him through.

Angel rode for eighteen hours. The wind beat against his face; the motor threatened to die more than once. His head ached, his back burned, but somewhere near dawn he saw the familiar shape of Pueblo rise up in front of him.

The motorcycle club welcomed him like a hero. They weighed his haul, whistled, clapped him on the back. Women came around. Joints passed from hand to hand. Bottles clinked.

Angel didn't really celebrate. The ghost of Crystal's last words and the image of two dead brothers on a store floor weighed more than the bag of drugs. He took a small peyote, hoping for clarity, but felt nothing—just a queasy stomach and a dull headache.

The next morning, his stash was gone. The club leader—everyone called him Chamuco—tossed him a bag of weed.

"That's your share," he said. "The rest stays here. You're not living off us for free."

Angel's anger flared. Before he could speak, he saw something that made his blood run cold: the man he'd killed in Chihuahua, standing behind Chamuco, cigarette in hand, shaking his head.

"You need to kill him," the apparition said calmly. "He has no respect. Take your bag and go. This place is not for you."

Angel didn't know if it was a hallucination, a product of the cave, the peyote, or his guilt. But the voice felt real.

He vaulted the counter, knife flashing. He drove the blade into Chamuco's neck. The man's hands flew up, eyes wide, blood blooming across his shirt.

The room exploded into shouting. Angel grabbed his bag and bolted out the back, heart slamming against his ribs. His bike keys were still inside. He jumped on Chamuco's motorcycle instead, kicked it to life and tore into the street.

A police cruiser spotted him almost immediately. The siren's wail cut through the morning quiet. For half an hour they danced: him gunning it down side roads, the cruiser gaining, losing, gaining again. Finally, the gas gauge hit empty. The engine coughed and died.

Angel coasted to a stop, hid his bag of drugs in some shrubs and raised his hands as the officers approached. This time, he didn't run.

Jail, the "Chihuahua Man" and Hallucinations

Jail shrank his world to concrete and steel. The walls sweated in winter. The mattress was thin, the blanket thinner. The air always smelled of sweat, disinfectant and something sour in the food you didn't want to identify.

The first night, as he tried to fall asleep to the chorus of snoring, cursing and rattling bars, he felt weight on his bunk. An inmate he didn't know clamped a hand over his mouth.

Panic surged. Angel remembered the sharpened toothbrush he'd hidden. He stabbed upward, again and again, feeling the resistance of muscle under skin. The man fell back cursing and stumbled out of the cell, leaving a smear of blood on the floor.

Angel sat on the bunk shaking, wiping his hands on his pants. Sleep didn't come. The morning day doors unlocked for breakfast, the body was now stiff and the blood was hardened, angel was tried and sentenced for this crime.

Days blurred. Meals slid through the slot at random hours. The only change in scenery came during brief walks in a small yard and talks shouted through bars.

The loneliness opened space in his head—and something moved into it. The man from Chihuahua, the one he'd seen behind Chamuco, started to appear more often. Angel called him "Chihuahua."

Sometimes he sat at the end of the bunk, smoking a cigarette that never burned down. Sometimes he leaned against the wall, arms crossed.

"You opened the door when you played with peyote," Chihuahua would say. "You wanted answers. You didn't say which kind."

Angel didn't know if he was losing his mind or gaining a companion. Either way, the hallucination kept him company.

To "tune in" the voice, he started cutting his forearms with anything sharp—plastic utensils, the metal edge of the food tray. The sting, the blood, the rush of adrenaline made Chihuahua sharper, like turning a radio dial until the static cleared.

Guards noticed the cuts and moved him to psych. After three years, a psychiatrist wrote that he was incompetent for part of his case and recommended transfer to a state mental hospital.

There, the bars turned into locked doors and security glass. Nurses wore scrubs. Med carts rolled down the halls. Angel swallowed pills that slowed his thoughts and blurred the edges of Chihuahua's voice, but never erased it.

He drew spirals and world trees in his notebook, attended group therapy where everyone introduced themselves by their diagnosis, and played cards with men who stared through the windows like they were watching a world they no longer had keys to.

One day a letter came. The envelope was neat, the handwriting feminine.

It was from Elena—his half-sister, his father's daughter from another marriage. He'd only met her once, at a funeral.

"When you get out, you can stay with me," she wrote. "I have a trailer in Pueblo East. Things are different now. I want to help you. Papá would want that."

The idea that someone still wanted him was enough to keep him breathing on the worst days.

Eventually, after enough time served and enough therapy boxes checked, he made parole

Elena's trailer in Pueblo East was small but clean. Kids' shoes by the door. Cartoon magnets on the fridge. A cross on the wall.

Her boyfriend, Jorge, seemed cool at first. He got Angel a job in construction. Angel hauled, mixed, carried, did whatever was asked. He kept his head down, took his meds, kept Chihuahua's voice to a low murmur.

It didn't take long to see the cracks. Jorge drank too much. When he was sober he could be funny and generous. When he was drunk he was controlling and mean—especially with Elena.

One Friday night, Jorge brought five coworkers home. They were drunk before they arrived. The kids hid in their bedroom. Elena warmed tortillas and meat, moving like a ghost through her own kitchen.

Jorge poured shots of tequila, bragging loudly about work. "My woman does what I say," he slurred, wrapping an arm around her neck a little too tight. She tried to pull away. He tightened his grip.

His boss whispered something in his ear. Jorge laughed and nodded.

"Let's show my friend how generous you are," he said, yanking Elena toward the bedroom.

Angel sat at the table with one of the workers, a guy named Chevo. His beer barely touched. He could hear Elena's muffled protests. One of the children peeked out, tears on their cheeks, then ducked back in.

Something inside Angel snapped into a familiar shape.

Chihuahua appeared behind Jorge in his mind's eye, the same way he'd appeared behind Chamuco.

"You're really going to just sit there?" the spirit asked quietly. "Another woman is screaming. Another family is broken. You know how this ends."

Angel grabbed a beer bottle, slammed it against the table until it shattered, leaving a jagged neck. His body moved before his mind could catch up.

He stormed into the small bedroom. Jorge looked up, hand on Elena's wrist, pants half undone. The boss stood nearby, belt off, a drunk grin on his face.

Angel slashed Jorge's neck. Blood spread across his shirt. The boss lunged, and the guys fell out, and Angel cut him across the stomach. The other men in the kitchen bolted through the door as shouting turned to screaming.

It was over in seconds, but the sound of Jorge choking on his own blood and Elena's ragged sobs stayed with Angel longer than any sentence.

He helped her pull her clothes together. She shook uncontrollably.

"I'm sorry," he whispered. "Esto no debía pasar."

He kissed her forehead. "Te quiero. You need to pick better men," he added, half joking, half begging her to choose another life.

He sat her and the kids on the couch, told them to lock the door and call the police once he was gone. He grabbed Jorge's car keys and walked out.

He drove until the lights of Pueblo shrank in the rearview mirror. The road turned black and empty again, like the one that had once led him south.

At some anonymous stretch of highway, he pulled over. The silence pressed on his ears. He opened the glove box and found a bottle of tablets.

He stared at them.

He thought of the people he'd killed. The lives he'd twisted: his own, his sister's, Crystal's. He remembered the cave, his father's face, Nana's hands, and the old curandero's stories. He was tired of carrying all of it.

He poured a handful of pills and swallowed them dry, then poured more. He washed them down with warm beer. It wouldn't kill him fast, but he didn't care. He wanted to drift out, away from flashing lights and court dates and ghosts.

Chihuahua appeared in the passenger seat, as usual.

"If you're going to die,at least do it right, the pills were antacid or at least open the trunk first," the spirit said.

Angel frowned. "The trunk?"

"There's something there your father left you. You want to spit on his memory by dying without even looking?" Your brother in law took the box, and wanted to burn it but never found time.

Annoyance cut through the fog of despair. Angel stepped out into the cold night, opened the trunk and started rooting through junk: an old jack, greasy rags, a coil of rope.

Then he saw it—a wooden box with a leather strap, worn but cared for. His chest tightened.

He pulled it out and set it under the dome light. His hands shook as he undid the strap.

Inside he found folded papers, yellowed with age, covered in neat handwriting and careful drawings. Recipes for salves, teas and poultices. Lists of plants and their uses. Geometric diagrams. Musical notations. Instructions for mixing peyote and mushrooms, prayers to saints and to old gods. At the bottom was a small pouch of dried herbs and seeds, and under that an envelope with his name.

The letter was from his father.

He wrote about Nana's knowledge and his own travels, about things he'd learned from curanderos and soldiers, about how their family line held both healing and darkness.

"Tu abuela era curandera," the letter said. "Tu abuelo, brujo. Tú tienes las dos cosas. This box is yours now. It can heal or destroy. You choose."

Angel's eyes burned.

He closed the box and set it on the passenger seat next to the ghost he could never quite get rid of.

The tablets sat like chalk in his stomach, but the urge to die had been replaced by a different weight: responsibility.

He turned the car around and drove toward the only place that had ever felt like a teacher and a judge at the same time.

Back to the mountain.
 Back to the cave.

Chihuahua led him, at least in his mind, up a misty path into the mountains. After hours of climbing, he reached a small shack with a door made of bamboo and rope.

An old man opened the door as if he'd been expecting him. His hair was white, his back a little bent, but his eyes were sharp.

"Pásale," he said. "I knew your grandfather. You took your time."

He poured tea for Angel, then set a shot of tequila on the table and nodded toward the empty space where Chihuahua usually hovered.

They sat. The old man began to talk.

He told Angel that in 1912 he and Angel's grandfather had met as street kids in Aguascalientes. Both fatherless. One surviving by picking pockets in a pulquería, the other wiping tables and sweeping floors.

One day General Panfilo's cavalry stormed into town recruiting men. The soldiers drank until they staggered. Angel's grandfather tried to steal from one and got caught. The old man joined the fight. Both were dragged outside and lined up against a mud wall to be shot.

The old man showed Angel a faded scar on his stomach. "The bullet went in here," he said. "They thought I was dead."

At the last moment Panfilo himself intervened. For some reason, he spared both boys and pressed them into his troops. They fought in the Mexican Revolution, rode under a sun that never seemed to set, saw men die for land and for pride.

Later they met Emiliano Zapata.

Zapata, the old man said, didn't just speak about land reform; he also spoke about ancient knowledge. He taught them about the nahualli—a person who learns the "four waters":

- Mathematics as a sacred language
- Cosmic geometry from the movement of stars
- Music that can revive or calm the soul
- Plants that can heal the body and open the mind

He explained the idea of the world tree connecting the underworld, earth and sky, its branches marking the four directions. He taught that humans belong to the earth, not the other way around.

"Then the Church and the government tried to erase everything," the old man said sadly. "They burned our books. They hanged our healers. Call us brujos."

He and Angel's grandfather fled through villages, learning from surviving shamans and curanderos, memorizing what they couldn't hide. The notes in the box were pieces of that journey—healing formulas mixed with darker experiments.

Angel stayed with the mountain curandero for five years. Every day he climbed the trail. Every night he descended.

He learned to recognize plants by smell, leaf shape, and where they grew. He learned which cured fever, which calmed nerves, which numbed pain, which opened doors in the mind. He learned limpias—cleansings with eggs, herbs, smoke and prayer.

He learned that some plants helped the body, some soothed the spirit, and some took you somewhere else entirely.

He drank tea that pulled him through what he described as "black holes" into other dimensions—places of colors and sounds where he understood everything and nothing at once. When he came back, hours had passed.

The old man nodded each time. "Eso, mijo. That place you go? That's where you return when this body dies. Where you choose what's next."

He taught Angel ceremonies with mushrooms: how to pick them respectfully, how to place them in a gourd, bless them with copal smoke, eat them in pairs on an empty stomach, and listen.

Later, he introduced him to el sapo—the desert toad. He showed him how to gently milk the venom from the glands, how to dry it into flaky crystals, and how a single inhalation could blast a person into a state where time disappeared.

Angel tried it once. He said he saw a universe made of light and heard a hum that was everything alive at once. When he came back, he was crying without knowing why.

"Shortest road to the gods," the curandero said. "Which is why you don't walk it too often."

Not all stories were cosmic. Some were ugly.

The old man spoke about battles during the revolution—trenches, mud, broken bodies. About comrades killing each other over gold. About watching a soldier shoot a curandera's amulet and laugh.

"That's when I understood," he told Angel, "saving knowledge might be more important than winning a war."

One morning, after years of this, Angel climbed the mountain and found the shed empty. No smoke from the fire, no footprints, no note.

It was like the mountain had swallowed the old man back.

Angel stood there a long time, the box of papers heavier than ever in his hands.

He took one last look at the valley, the trail, the sky, and decided it was time to go north again.

Back to Pueblo.
 Back to the mess he'd left behind

Back in Colorado, Angel stopped at a payphone outside a gas station. He punched in Elena's number from memory. She answered on the second ring.

"¿Bueno?"

"Elena… soy yo, Angel."

There was a long pause. Then a shaky, "¿Dónde estás?"

They talked briefly. She gave him her address. He said he'd come by.

When he got there, he didn't pull into the driveway. He parked half a block away and watched.

Elena was in the yard, playing tag with two kids—his niece and nephew. Their laughter floated down the street. Potted geraniums sat on the steps. The house looked small but cared for.

She looked happy. Not rich. Not safe from every bad thing. But I'm happy.

He smelled his own clothes—sweat, smoke, earth. The box of formulas sat in the passenger seat, covered with a blanket. His hands were scarred. His face looked older than his years in the side mirror.

What was he going to do? Knock on the door and say, "Hi, I've killed three people but I also studied plants on a mountain and want redemption"?

He watched for a while. His chest hurt. Then he wiped his eyes with the back of his hand, put the car in gear, and left.

Three blocks later, red and blue lights lit up the inside of the car.

Expired plates. Broken tail light. No insurance. No ID.

They pulled him out. Searched the vehicle. The warrants and old charges lit up their screens like a Christmas tree. Within minutes, the quiet end of the street was full of cruisers.

In court, his past and present collided. Witnesses. Old files. New charges. He was given three sentences of twenty-five years each.

Back to orange.
 Back to concrete.
 Back to Chihuahua's voice bouncing off the cell walls.

He did his time. Fought when he had to. Survived a shower attack with another sharpened toothbrush. Spent nights talking to a ghost and days trying to keep his head down.

After twenty-five years, they decided he was more mentally ill than actively dangerous. They moved him to a mental rehabilitation center in Wheat Ridge.

There, he traded cell bars for locked doors and paper cups of pills. Therapists asked about childhood, Nana, his father, the cave, the killings. He told pieces. Never everything. The missing parts he kept for his conversations with Chihuahuas.

He was given a release date: June 18, 2020.

He wrote it over and over on scrap paper. 18–6–20. Turned the numbers into spirals. Drew world trees sprouting out of them.

Then the world outside shut down. A new virus. Lockdowns. Delays.

His papers sat somewhere on someone's desk, buried under forms and excuses.

By early 2022, decades of smoking and stress caught up to him. Walking up the short flight of stairs to the day room left him breathless. He coughed until he tasted iron.

One night he woke up, gasping like someone was sitting on his chest. Orderlies rushed in, wheeled him down a fluorescent hallway. Machines beeped. Oxygen hissed.

He lay in a hospital bed, tubes in his arms, mask over his face, monitors tracing his fading heartbeat. The room smelled like antiseptic and plastic.

The Chihuahua sat near his feet, watching quietly.

For the first time, Angel didn't have the energy to talk back.

He closed his eyes and thought of Nana's clay house. The sound of her comal. His father's rough hand on his shoulder. The cool, wet air of the cave, the echo of water drops. The mountain curandero's stories about cosmic trees and recycled lives.

He thought of Crystal,the only love he ever had and wondered what would've been of them two, then rain falling straight down, rinsing mud off their clothes while they laughed.

He wondered if there really was another dimension waiting—one where his father, Nana, maybe even the old curandero stood by a world tree and asked him what he'd learned.

The machines hummed. Nurses checked vitals and wrote numbers on a chart. No family waited by his side. No kids held his hand.

Angel died quietly in that sterile room.

His body went to a morgue, then somewhere else. There was no funeral. In a cardboard box labeled with his prison number, his father's letter and the curandero's notes gathered dust.

Elena never knew he'd once watched her from a car, then driven away because he decided he didn't deserve to knock. Her kids grew up without knowing they had an uncle who'd tried—clumsily, violently, and too late—to protect their mother.

Years later, sitting on a bench outside a mental hospital during smoke breaks, I listened to Angel's story. To most people, he was just another criminal who died locked up.

To me, he was something more complicated: a man born between healer and sorcerer, between Pueblo and Chihuahua, between reality and visions—someone who wanted redemption and never quite found the door.

Dog Boy

Chapter 2

It was October 1984. Leaves were falling in slow spirals, Halloween decorations slapped against rusty trailer walls, and kids in plastic masks ran through the thin snow of a dangerous, low-income park on the edge of town.

Rookie officer Francisco Pacheco, also a reservist in the National Guard, was on his first patrol alone. For months he'd been the guy in the passenger seat, watching, listening, taking notes. Now, because the department was short-staffed, he was in the driver's seat with a radio, a badge, and a town that didn't care he was new.

When the 911 call came in—"strong chemical smell, maybe drugs"—most officers ignored it. That park always smelled like something: burning trash, space heaters, gasoline, desperation. There were "more important calls," they said.

But Pacheco was still green enough to take everything personally. He turned the wheel and headed for the trailer park.

Snow and slush made the narrow roads slick. Kids darted between cars, masks crooked, pillowcases of candy swinging from their hands. He drove slow, scanning numbers on faded tin until he finally found the lot from the CAD notes.

A bright but peeling yellow trailer sat behind a sagging chain-link fence. The small gate squeaked when he pushed it open. The wooden steps groaned under his boots as he climbed to the door and knocked.

A shrill bark exploded from the other side, followed by slow, heavy footsteps.

An overweight woman opened the door, dragging an oxygen tank behind her. The plastic tubes dug into her cheeks. In her arms, a bug-eyed chihuahua shook and barked at something over her shoulder.

Her voice was high-pitched and breathless. "You're the first one to actually show up," she said. "I've been calling and calling."

"Ma'am, I'm Officer Pacheco," he said, already pulling out his notebook. "You reported a chemical smell?"

She stepped aside. "It's freezing out there. Come in. I can't walk back and forth."

He stepped into a two-bedroom, one-bath trailer that smelled like dog urine, cigarettes, and fried food. A worn red couch with cigarette burns faced a TV. A fishtank bubbled in the corner. A narrow bar separated the living room from the tiny kitchen. To his right a short hall led to a bathroom and two bedrooms. The walls, once white, were tobacco yellow.

The woman, easily 600 pounds, shuffled back to the couch. The chihuahua hopped into her lap, still barking and shaking, its eyes bulging with constant anxiety. Her enormous chest wobbled with every breath. She pulled off her oxygen line, coughed, then tried to smile.

"As you can see, officer, I got trouble moving around," she said, chest wheezing. "I only go out for doctors' appointments. I grew up in this trailer. My mama left it to me."

"How long have you been smelling chemicals?" Pacheco asked, pen hovering.

"Couple months," she said. "Smells like when my nephew was cooking that stuff. Meth." She scratched the dog's head. "I'd come back from the doctor and the house would stink. One day I found him

29

smoking it right here in the living room. Kicked him out that same day."

"What's your nephew's name?"

"Jason."

"And now?"

"Now I smell it when I crack the window to let some air in," she said. "Not as strong, but it's there. I know that smell. I'm worried about the kids in this neighborhood."

He wrote it all down: name, description, history. "Anything else you want to add?"

She shook her head, out of breath. He slid the notebook back into his pocket.

"I'll do what I can to keep an eye on the area," he told her. "And I'll see what I can find out about the smell."

Outside, his breath smoked in the air. He drove slow loops around the park, but every trailer had steam rising from heating vents. In the cold, every home exhaled something. There were almost two hundred units; the park was a maze of aluminum and mud.

No obvious lab. No suspect. Just a rookie with a notebook and a promise he wasn't sure he could keep.

Days turned into weeks. Weeks slid into months. The park fell quiet—or maybe the rest of the city just got louder.

He noticed new oxygen tanks stacked precariously on the yellow trailer's porch. No one came out to bring them in. One afternoon, the sight of four full tanks leaning against the steps bothered him enough to stop.

He knocked. The chihuahua barked, high and frantic. No answer.

He knocked again. On the third knock, the door creaked open.

The smell hit him first.

Rot. Sweet and heavy, unmistakable. It crawled up his nose and settled in his throat. Every cop knew that smell after the first few calls. It was something your brain never forgot.

"Police!" he called. "Anyone home?"

He stepped inside.

Rose—he remembered her name then—was on the red couch. Or what was left of her. Her face was swollen and discolored, a sick blend of purple and green. Her legs were covered in moving white threads of maggots. In places the skin had been chewed away down to bone.

The chihuahua sat on her chest, teeth working at a ragged edge of flesh. When Pacheco entered, the dog paused, growled around its mouthful, then went back to eating.

He clamped a hand over his nose and mouth, trying not to gag.

He backed out, radioed for backup and the coroner, then took one more breath and forced himself back inside to make sure no one else was in danger.

Just him. The dog. The silent TV.

As he turned to leave, movement flashed in the corner of his eye. A window on the side of the trailer banged open and a thin young white man scrambled out, landing in the snow and sprinting for the back fence.

"Police! Stop!" Pacheco shouted, instincts taking over.

He jumped off the porch and chased the runner down the narrow strip of yard. The guy hit the chain-link fence, trying to scramble over, but Pacheco tackled him mid-climb. They hit the ground hard. The kid thrashed, mumbling nonsense and grinding his teeth.

Up close, he reeked of sweat and chemicals. His jaw worked nonstop. His pupils were huge, his eyes unfocused. He muttered to himself under his breath, lost in a private storm.

By the time backup arrived, the young man was cuffed and sitting in the back of Pacheco's car, twitching and talking to nobody. They decided to hold him until he sobered up enough for questioning.

Inside the trailer, the coroner and his assistant worked in paper masks and gloves. One of them yelped when the chihuahua bit his ankle.

"Get this damn dog out of here," he snapped. "We can't work with him chewing on the patient."

Pacheco borrowed an extra mask and gloves, walked back into the thick smell, and scooped up the snarling chihuahua. As he carried the dog toward the back bedroom, he noticed a mattress on the floor, a digital scale, little jewelry baggies, an incense pipe blackened with residue, and a bent spoon resting in a soda cap. The air was flavored with burned chemicals.

Jason's room.

He dropped the dog inside, shut the door, and turned the lock.

Two minutes later the coroner and his assistant came down the squeaking stairs, peeling off their gear.

"We need detectives," the coroner said flatly. "This isn't natural. Multiple stab wounds in her back."

Everyone went quiet. They'd assumed her weight and health had caught up with her. They hadn't expected murder.

One of the officers called it in. As they secured the scene, Pacheco drove the young man—Jason—to the station. The plan was simple: let him detox, then ask why he slipped out Rose's window while she was rotting on the couch.

Forty-eight hours later, Pacheco walked Jason from the cell to an interview room. The kid looked smaller now, like the drugs had burned off and left nothing but a tired, scared skeleton.

Detective Joe, a veteran with coffee-stained teeth and calm eyes, waited with a folder in front of him. They Mirandized Jason again. This time he nodded that he understood.

Tears lined his eyes before they even asked the first question.

"Can I get the death penalty?" he blurted, voice shaking. "I don't wanna live any more."

"Start from the beginning," Joe said. "Tell us what happened. Step by step."

Jason stared at the table. His fingers picked at a nonexistent thread.

"It was cold," he said. "I'd been up for three days, high on meth and drinking to beat the cold. Sleeping in a cave some kids dug in the hill after my aunt kicked me out. I knew if I didn't quit, I was gonna end up dead or here. Guess I was right."

He swallowed hard.

"I went to my plug," he continued. "Gave him my bike and a watch I stole from my dad. He fronted me an eight ball and some baggies. I still had my scale at my aunt's. My plan was to cut it, sell it, feed my habit, maybe get a motel room for a night."

He described slipping through the broken window, tripping over his deflating air mattress, unpacking the drugs. He talked about

33

measuring three one-gram baggies and leaving half a gram in the spoon.

"My aunt was always in her room or on that couch," he said. "I figured I'd be in and out before she even knew."

But the chihuahua barked and woke her.

"I heard her yelling," Jason said, voice going flat as he quoted her. "'That better not be you, Jason! I told you to get the fuck out and never come back!'"

She struggled to her feet, using her walker. He could hear her heavy steps coming down the hall toward his room as he cooked the meth in the spoon. When it cooled, he injected it.

"It hit me like a truck," he said. "Head rush. It felt like my chest was on fire and my brain left my body."

Through the high, he heard her say, "I'm calling the cops."

"In my head," Jason whispered, "she turned into a monster. Like, really. I wasn't in that trailer any more, I was in some other place. If she called the cops, I thought I was done. Locked up forever. Something snapped."

His face crumpled.

"I came out behind her before she reached the phone," he said. "I grabbed a knife from the kitchen. I don't even remember grabbing it. It was just in my hand."

He talked about stabbing her from behind, again and again, until she slid onto the couch.

"The last thing I remember from that high is thinking, 'I slayed the monster,'" he said, tears running down his cheeks. "Then I went back to my room and smoked a bowl. Next thing I know, two days passed. I walked out, saw her on the couch... and I knew what I'd done."

He admitted taking whatever he could carry from her room—jewelry, a TV, anything to trade for more meth. He traded the knife too. Then he stayed in the cave, dealing and shooting up, until Pacheco knocked.

Jason pled guilty. The judge gave him twenty-five years to life.

Three years later, another call came from the same trailer park.

Someone was bleeding in the middle of the street.

Firefighters arrived first, then patrol cars, then the ambulance that mostly served as a hearse. The victim was a man named Joseph, a quiet pizza worker who lived alone in one of the park's smallest trailers.

Five bullets in the back, the paramedics said. The coroner later added another detail: Joseph's veins showed signs of massive meth injection, and his body bore marks of torture and sexual assault. His wrists and ankles had indentations like zip-ties had been there. He had been hurt for a while before he died.

No one heard anything but a few pops. No one saw anything but shadows. Nothing about Joseph's life explained why he had been turned into an enemy.

The case was going cold within days.

Now Detective Pacheco—no longer a rookie, but still hungry—was handed the file. He did everything they taught him at the academy: walked the scene, canvassed neighbors, traced Joseph's work, his routine, his few known friends.

Nothing obvious. Just another dead body in a place the city didn't care about.

He went back to the beginning, back to the park's old ghosts, and thought of Jason.

Maybe the kid knew something about the neighborhood that wasn't written in any report.

He went to the prison with a deal on the table: help us, and maybe we could talk to the DA about shaving some time.

Jason was sober now, in that hollow, worn-out kind of way. Sobriety had carved deeper lines into his face. He listened, then nodded slowly.

"You really wanna know, detective?" Jason asked. "Then listen."

He told him about the Martinez family.

How they controlled the park's meth trade. How Chuy—the uncle—ran everything from a main trailer, with Doberman dogs he bred and sold on the side. How his nephew Neto acted as muscle, dealer, and problem-solver, living in the trailer next door. How a girlfriend named Ashley floated in and out when she wasn't fighting with Neto.

He described five trailers tied to their operation:

1. Chuy's main house.
2. Neto's place, with random cousins and Ashley.
3. A stash/cooking trailer.
4. A "party" trailer where people came to buy and use.
5. A strange back trailer where dogs barked, a van came once a week, and nobody in the park really knew what went on.

"If somebody killed Joseph," Jason said, "it was probably them. Everybody knows this."

"You knew Joseph?" Pacheco asked.

Jason nodded. "Yeah. He was that weird quiet dude. I worked at the pizza place. No friends. Kids threw rocks at him, called him 'pedo' just because he kept to himself. Last trailer behind the fifth Martinez place. If he saw something he wasn't supposed to, they'd handle it."

"Thank you," Pacheco said. "We'll see what we can do with this."

He walked straight from the prison to the DA's office to get search warrants. The judge denied them: too thin, too circumstantial.

The case, officially, stayed cold.

Unofficially, it burrowed into Pacheco's chest like a splinter.

He kept patrolling the park more than anyone else, telling himself he was honoring the promise he'd made to Rose years earlier. Friday nights, like Jason suggested, he'd cruise through and watch people drift in and out of the Martinez trailers.

One of those nights, he saw a woman in her early twenties, a ginger who looked twice her age, screaming outside Neto's place. Drunk, high, or both.

"I'll go to the police, motherfucker!" she yelled at the door. "I'll tell them all about Joseph and Chuy!"

The door opened. A thin, bald Mexican man ran out, slapped her hard across the face, and sent her sprawling onto the icy street.

"Shut up, bitch, or I'll kill you," he said, then turned and went back inside.

The woman—Ashley—walked away, wiping blood from her mouth, muttering under her breath. She passed right by Pacheco's unmarked car.

"You need help?" he asked through the window.

"Fuck you, man," she snapped, stumbling past.

He got out, stepped into her path. "Ma'am, I'm Officer Pacheco with Pueblo West PD."

She rolled her eyes. "Uhu. And what do you want me to do?"

"I heard what you said," he replied. "We can press charges. We can talk. But only if you want to."

She walked ten steps, stopped, then spun around.

"What do I get if I talk?" she asked.

"What do you want?"

"My warrant to go away."

His face fell a little. "I'll see what I can do," he said honestly.

At the station, they put her in an interview room. She sat, pulled at the frayed hem of her shorts—and something small and glass fell from her waistband and shattered on the floor. An oil burner. Meth pipe.

Police searched her and found more.

She was bleeding from a cut on her leg, high as a kite. Per policy, they booked her in possession. The interview would wait.

Five minutes later, alarms screamed inside the jail. Guards ran for the bathrooms. Pacheco followed.

Jason lay on the scummy tile, covered in blood. He'd been stabbed over forty times with a shank that disappeared as quickly as it had been used. No one had seen anything. No one had heard anything.

It looked like a message.

With a key witness dead and no clean *way* to explain his connection to Ashley, Internal Affairs pulled Pacheco off the case. Too many "errors in judgment," they said. Too much contamination.

He nodded through the reprimand, heard the words, and walked out of the building feeling like someone had slammed a door in his face.

The case gnawed at him anyway.

Two weeks of vacation appeared in the system—mandatory, they called it. He used them in the park.

He took an old seized van, flattened one tire, stocked up on food and water, and turned himself into a surveillance camera with a heartbeat.

He watched the Martinez trailers for days. Friday, Saturday, Sunday—just traffic, deals, arguments, nothing that would convince any judge.

He smelled his own sweat, his own fear, his own embarrassment at what he was doing. The empty bottles rolled on the floor. Bushes next to the van served as his bathroom. The thin line between dedication and obsession blurred.

He kept telling himself: If nothing's here, I can walk away. If something's here, I can't.

Then he saw the panel van.

Then he saw the little girl run.

Then he watched her get dragged back inside.

And then everything changed.

The raid on the Martinez property came at dawn, a swarm of flashing lights and shouting boots. With the warrant finally signed, twenty officers moved like a wave through the park, hitting trailers one, two, three, and five all at once.

Trailer five felt colder than the morning air.

Pacheco's shoulder hit the door alongside the battering ram. On the second strike, the frame gave way. Light and sound flooded into a space that hadn't been seen either in any real way for a long, long time.

Chains clinked. People flinched.

The main room was packed with bodies—men and women shackled to pipes, bed frames, each other. Their skin was pale under dirt. Ankles and wrists were raw. Some of them cried, some just stared. Most looked too exhausted to even be afraid.

"Multiple victims—get medics, now," someone yelled behind him.

Pacheco's eyes swept the room, counting faces, counting chains. Every person there had been a rumor once. A story. "Somebody's cousin never made it past the border." Now they had names, scars, and eyes that tracked him like he might vanish if they blinked.

He felt guilt crawl up his spine.

How long have you been here while I drove past? he thought. How many times did I look the other way because it was just 'a drug park'?

The chorus of barking led him down the hall.

At the last door, the sound was deafening—dogs slamming into walls, claws scratching at wood, frantic howls and snarls rising over each other like a storm.

He kicked the door open.

The smell of feces, urine, and wet fur punched him in the face.

Dogs crowded the small room. Big ones, small ones, mutts, purebreds, matted and thin. Chain links rattled where they were tied to improvised posts. Their eyes shone yellow in the dim light.

In the middle of them, chained to the wall by a metal collar around his neck, crouched a boy.

He was maybe eight years old. Naked, filthy, knees and elbows scabbed. His hair hung in greasy tangles around his face.

He was on all fours.

When Pacheco entered, the boy bared his teeth and barked.

Not a word. Not a cry for help. A raw, animal bark, loud and high and terrified.

For a second, Pacheco's brain refused to label him human. The posture, the sound, the wildness in his eyes—everything said "animal." Then he saw the small hands curled on the stained floor. The collar digging into thin skin. The ribs marking his sides.

His throat closed.

He holstered his gun.

"Hey," he said softly, as if talking to a scared dog. "Hey, buddy. It's okay. We're not here to hurt you."

The boy's gaze flicked between his face and his hands, reading more in his body language than his words. One of the dogs stepped between them, growling. The boy mirrored the dog's stance, low and defensive.

Behind him, an officer whispered, "What the hell… they chained him like one of them."

Pacheco didn't answer. His mind split in two: one part cataloguing evidence, another part screaming quietly inside.

He remembered Rose, alone on her couch. Jason, sobbing and begging for the needle. Joseph, in the street. All of them connected now to this boy chained in the dark, a living piece of the Martinez operation.

This is what we let happen when we write people off as junkies and illegals, he thought bitterly. This is what grows in the cracks.

"Get Animal Control and paramedics for the kid," he said. "We're going to need both."

It took time to get the dogs separated and the chain off the boy's neck. He fought them at first, screaming, biting, thrashing, convinced his "pack" was being stolen. Every human hand felt like a threat. Every raised voice sounded like the day the cops kicked the door in.

Later, they would call him "Michael" in the paperwork.

To Pacheco, he would always be "the dog-boy from trailer five."

In the months and years that followed, Michael's story unfolded in case files and whispered conversations.

No birth certificate. No hospital record. According to Neto's eventual testimony, he'd been born three months early in Chuy's living room, while his mother Mary was deep in heroin use.

"Nobody thought he'd make it," Neto told detectives later. "He did. That was the first surprise."

He was raised in filth and chaos. Fed on whatever was handy, often dog food. Allowed to drink from whatever the dogs drank from. When customers came with money, they petted the Dobermans and stepped over the boy. When they came with violence, he watched what "love" looked like in that house: hands, belts, fear.

The "Carnicería" trailer, Neto said, was where undocumented migrants who couldn't pay were held. Ransom calls went out. If money didn't come, people wouldn't live. Dogs were always fed. Boxes were always carried out.

"I tried not to go in there," Neto said. "The smell… I didn't want that in my head. But the kid, he lived in it. That was his world. Blood, barking, people screaming."

Child protective services tried to place Michael in foster homes after the raid. He didn't understand chairs, forks, or bedtime stories. He understood corners, concrete floors, and growling. He ate off the ground if no one stopped him. He panicked if he couldn't hear dogs.

When someone raised their voice, he flinched like he'd been hit.

When someone raised their hand too fast, he bit.

By twelve he'd spent more time in juvenile detention and short-term facilities than in any home. Clinical notes were full of words like developmental delay, attachment disorder, complex trauma.

Pacheco kept tabs from a distance. It wasn't his job anymore, but he couldn't help it. The boy he'd found barking in that room had etched himself into his mind.

Whenever he was near the county office, he'd ask, "Hey, you guys still got that kid from trailer five on your radar?" Sometimes someone would shrug. Sometimes a social worker would sigh and say, "He's in another placement," or, "He ran again."

Years passed.

Michael turned eighteen. Then twenty. Then thirty. The system let him go in the way systems do—with a handful of paperwork and not enough support.

He drifted to the edges. Homeless camps. Train yards. The places that smell of smoke and fear.

Then the rapes started.

Men and women assaulted near rail lines in different towns, the attacker wearing a dog mask or covering his face, rarely speaking. Victims described a heavy man who moved like someone used to sleeping outside—fast, quiet, cautious.

DNA tied the cases together.

The assaults were violent, chaotic, and senseless. Not the calculated cruelty of Chuy's cartel deals, but something more twisted: a man whose ideas of closeness, power, and fear had been welded together in one broken shape.

When Neto agreed to cooperate for a sentence reduction, he painted in the rest.

"Michael doesn't know what normal is," he said. "He learned that touching means pain, that screaming is part of it. He ain't stupid, but he ain't right either. You let that loose with no help? What do you think's gonna happen?"

They found Michael living in a tent by the railroad tracks with a pack of dogs, just like Neto said they would. When they approached, the dogs guarded him. He moved to stand in front of them, shoulders hunched, eyes wary.

He didn't fight when they cuffed him. He just looked confused and scared, like someone who's been dragged into a kind of light that hurts his eyes.

Psychiatrists later wrote that he had schizophrenia, borderline traits, cognitive disability, and a lifelong history of extreme abuse. He didn't fully grasp consent or personal boundaries. In his interviews, when he talked at all, he called some of his victims "friends."

"I showed them love," he said once, flat and earnest.

It made Pacheco sick to his stomach.

The jury still found him guilty.

In prison, Michael was not seen as a damaged boy from trailer five. He was seen as a rapist. Other inmates attacked him. He was stabbed, beaten, left with scars inside and out. After multiple assaults, the state moved him to a psychiatric facility in Jefferson County.

Pacheco could have let the story end there.

Instead, he found himself dialing the hospital every few months. "You still have a patient named Michael?" he'd ask. "From the Pueblo case?"

Sometimes the answer was yes. Sometimes a nurse would say, "He's calmer on this new medication," or, "He had a bad week, tore up his room." Once, a tech told him, "He doesn't talk much, but when the therapy dogs come in, he just sits with them. Puts his forehead against theirs. Won't move."

In 2020, talk began of discharging some long-term patients into the community with strict conditions. Pacheco, nearing retirement, argued quietly that Michael should remain under heavy supervision.

The doctors said the laws didn't allow indefinite confinement when a patient showed some capacity to live outside, especially with medication and support.

"The boy was made in a monster's house," one psychiatrist said gently. "He didn't make himself. We can't fix the past, but we have to work with the present."

The last time Pacheco saw Michael was by accident.

He was off duty, driving past a bus stop near the clinic. A large man with a worn jacket stood there, a plastic grocery bag in one hand. A woman stood next to him, talking. She laughed at something he tried to say.

Michael smiled back—awkward, lopsided, but real.

A small child tugged at his coat, swinging from his sleeve. Michael looked down and ruffled the kid's hair with a big, careful hand.

Pacheco slowed the car, heart thudding.

He recognized the eyes.

The boy from trailer five. Now a father. Waiting for a bus like any other tired working-class man.

He didn't pull over. He didn't bang on the glass. He just watched them climb into the bus, watched the doors close, watched the taillights disappear.

He sat there a long moment with the engine idling, hands on the steering wheel, staring at the empty bus stop.

Relief and dread twisted together in his chest.

Relief that someone so broken had found some fragment of ordinary life: a woman, a child, a job at Safeway, a pharmacy that gave him his meds.

Dread because he knew how thin that safety net was—one missed appointment, one bad day, one system failure away from another headline.

Years later, when Detective Francisco Pacheco finally turned in his gun and badge, people asked him which cases he remembered most. They expected the big ones—the cartel busts, the hostage situations, the high-speed chases.

Instead, his mind always went back to the trailer park.

To Rose, alone on her red couch.

To Jason, crying in an interview room, begging for a punishment he thought he deserved.

To Joseph, facedown in the snow between two rusted trailers.

And to a boy chained in the dark with the dogs, barking at him in terror.

Those were the ghosts that retired with him.

Those were the stories that made him realize monsters aren't born in caves or jungles.

They're built, piece by piece, in places everyone else has decided not to look.

Colorado Cannibal

Chapter 3

It was September 2020, when the hot days finally started letting go of the Front Range and gray skies began to hang over Colorado. I sat on the far side of the X-ray room glass with my hands over my mouth, elbows on my knees, staring at the glowing monitors.

On the other side of the glass, the tech slid a film aside and brought up a new image. A skull appeared in shades of white and gray. Just above the left temple, a shadow bloomed like a dark flower in winter.

The tech glanced back at me and whispered, "I'm sorry."

I already knew about the tumor. It was written in his chart in dry medical language: slow-growing mass, frontal lobe. But knowing it on paper and seeing it on the screen weren't the same. On the monitor it looked like something coiled inside his head.

David, almost a century old, was sitting on the table, half undressed. White hair, white beard, skin so thin it seemed almost transparent, webbed with blue veins. His hands shook as he pulled his shirt back over his shoulders. The bones of his wrists looked sharp enough to cut through the fabric.

He didn't ask for help. Pride kept him moving in careful, stubborn motions until he was dressed.

Outside the hospital, the sky was a flat sheet of gray. David squinted at it like he was trying to remember something.

"Denny's," he said.

"Now?" I asked.

He gave me a look like "Of course now, " then added, "Strawberry malt."

No "please." No question mark at the end. Just an old man's order, heavy with a lifetime of expecting obedience.

I drove him there in the facility van. He walked in slowly, leaning on my arm, then slid into a booth as if he'd done the same thing for seventy years. When the malt arrived, he drank it in small pulls through the straw, eyes half-closed, as if sweetness was a temporary truce with everything else.

When he finished, he tapped the glass with a crooked finger.

"One more. To go."

Back in the van, the road hummed under us. I watched his profile: sharp nose, sunken cheeks, watery eyes. Somewhere behind that thin skull and bruised flesh was the man his file described. I thought of the words I had read:

Rape. Murder. Cannibalism. Pedophilia.
Borderline Personality Disorder. Bipolar Disorder.
'Self-reported' victim count: 80+.

I couldn't reconcile that file with the trembling figure beside me, sipping the last of a strawberry malt.

So I asked him.

"David," I said quietly, "if you could give me one piece of advice—just one—for someone younger… what would it be?"

He sucked at the straw for a moment, thinking. Then he swallowed and said:

"Don't do criminal stuff."

There was no humor in his voice. Just flat, tired certainty.

"Once you start," he went on, "there's no going back. Your record's never erased. And if you are doing it, don't get caught—'cause you ain't a criminal till they grab you. After that, that's all you'll ever be."

I stared at the road ahead. That sentence hung between us like a bad smell.

After a moment I asked the thing that had been sitting at the back of my throat since I read his file.

"If you could start your life again… what would you change?"

He stopped drinking.

His jaw tightened. He stared straight ahead, neck stiff, eyes not really seeing the highway. When he finally answered, the words came out dry and scraped:

"I wish…" he paused, swallowing, "I wish I never became the thing they said I was."

His fingers tightened on the paper cup.

"I wish I'd had a different beginning."

For a second, the monster in his file disappeared, and I saw only an old man who knew he had wasted every chance life had ever given him.

I didn't know it then, but that was the moment a door opened. Not for forgiveness—he never asked for that—but for explanation.

Because David wasn't born in a hospital bed with a tumor and a criminal record.

He came from somewhere.

And that somewhere—if you believe him—started long before him, in the mountains, in winter, when hunger made people do things they never wanted written down.

The Files and the Silence

Before he talked, his papers did.

At the facility, every resident had a file. Most were thin. David's was a brick: a century's worth of diagnoses, transfers, disciplinary reports, court transcripts, police photos, nurses' notes, and scribbled addenda from doctors who had tried to understand him and eventually gave up.

I read it in pieces. Lunch breaks. Night shifts. Early mornings before he woke up.

Diagnoses stamped over decades:

- Borderline Personality Disorder
- Bipolar Disorder I
- Post-Traumatic Stress Disorder (combat-related)
- Possible organic brain changes (tumor, frontal lobe)
- History of alcohol dependence
- History of sexual deviancy and violent fantasies

The language was clinical, but the picture was simple: a brain scarred by trauma, destabilized by mood swings, possibly warped further by a tumor growing slowly in the dark.

A few notes stuck with me:

1979, prison intake:
"Inmate expresses little remorse. State killing feels 'calming' and 'natural.' Appears dissociated when describing violence."

1984, psychological evaluation:
"Emotional responses are inconsistent. At times flat, at times

childlike curiosity, at times inappropriate laughter when discussing harm to others."

2005, state mental facility nursing note:
 "The patient refuses group therapy. Says others 'smell like fear.' Requested raw meat instead of breakfast."

In one margin, a psychiatrist had written:

"Patient states: 'I wasn't born this way.'"

That line matched what he'd said in the van: I wish I'd had a different beginning.

His criminal record, in cold ink:

- Confirmed homicide victim: 1
- Strongly suspected victims: 6–12
- Self-reported victim count: "Over 80."

Next to that last line, someone had scribbled: Likely exaggeration; pathological storyteller.

Maybe it was. Maybe it wasn't. There are always bodies nobody finds and crimes nobody writes reports about. What mattered to me wasn't the exact number—it was that even at the end of his life, David still carried that number inside his head.

He didn't speak about his past at first. For months, we went to appointments and Denny's and back to the ward in silence. I cared for his body—his meds, his food, his diapers—while his mind stayed sealed.

Every now and then, something slipped.

One afternoon I was taking his blood pressure and he stared at my wristwatch.

"Quartz?" he croaked.

"Yeah," I said.

He nodded slightly.

"My father hated clocks," he murmured.

I waited. He closed his eyes and shut down again.

"Later," he said.

And later finally came.

Blood in the Snow (His Grandfather's Story)

It started after seven months of malts and appointments and half-finished sentences. We were in our usual booth at Denny's. He had his strawberry malt. I had coffee I wasn't really drinking.

He put his straw down, wiped his moustache with the back of his hand and said:

"You read my file."

"I read what they wrote," I answered.

He nodded slowly.

"Then I should tell you what they didn't."

He leaned back. His eyes drifted somewhere else—far past the parking lot, past Colorado, past his own lifetime.

"My story doesn't start with me," he said. "It starts in the mountains. With my grandfather. He told my father. My father told me. Then I lived it all over again in my own way."

He took a breath and slipped into the past.

"They came west in the 1800s," he began. "From Springfield to California. Same time as the others—the ones they wrote about. The snow, the wagons, the dead."

He never used the name "Donner Party," but everything he described matched the stories historians tell about those trapped on the wrong side of the Sierras. Whether his grandfather really belonged to that exact wagon train or one like it, no one can prove now. But David believed it. And he believed the hunger they carried forward was real.

"At first," he said, "it was a big adventure. New land, new sky. My grandfather was young then—strong, tall, used to working with cattle and horses. He worked for a rich family, driving animals and helping with the wagons.

They followed a man who swore he knew a faster way through the mountains. He didn't. They lost time. The path was bad—rocks, narrow passes, places where the wagons had to be taken apart and dragged. People started leaving things behind. Furniture. Tools. Memories.

Then the snow came.

Not pretty snow. Not the dusting you get in town. Walls of it. Piling against the wagons, burying the animals. The trail disappeared. The food ran out.

They killed the weak cattle first. Boiled bones, ate hide. People got quiet. You could hear stomachs growling louder than voices.

They made camp by a frozen lake. Cabins thrown together from logs, tarps, and prayer. The smell inside—wet wool, unwashed bodies, sickness. Outside, the wind howled all night. Inside, children cried in their sleep.

Then people started to die.

Some from sickness. Some from the cold. Some just… gave up. Lay down and let the snow and hunger swallow them.

At first they buried the bodies. Then the ground got too hard. Then they stacked them outside the cabins. Then they stopped burying them at all.

My grandfather told my father there was a day when he looked at a frozen body and didn't see a person anymore. He saw meat.

They tried to fight it. He said that. Said they tried. But the children's ribs were showing, and the mothers were crying without tears, and the men were walking like ghosts.

Somebody took a knife. He said he never forgot the sound it made cutting into frozen flesh. Not the taste either. After that, it was easier to do it again.

When the rescuers finally came, they found pots on the fire that didn't smell like any animal they knew. They found bones stripped clean. Dead mixed with the living.

My grandmother survived. So did my grandfather. Her first husband didn't. His organs were found in one of those pots.

They never forgot that winter. They moved to California, changed their names, and tried to become normal. But my grandfather told my father: 'No meat tastes like that. None fills you up the same.'"

David's voice went quiet for a moment.

"He passed that hunger on," he said finally. "Not in blood alone. In stories. On the way he taught my father to cut meat. The way he looked at people when he thought no one saw."

He looked at me then, eyes cloudy.

"So you see," he said, "by the time I was born, the recipe was already written. I just followed it."

The Shed (His Father's Hunts)

"By the time I came along," David continued, "it was California, 1932. Farms, dust, the tail end of the Depression. Nobody had enough. Some had nothing at all."

He shifted in the booth, bones protesting, memories not.

"My father grew up in the shadow of that cabin in the snow," he said. "He'd never been there, but he'd heard every inch of it in his daddy's stories. He was the oldest boy, the only son. That meant he carried the secret.

On the outside, he was just a farmhand. Worked at a local ranch, did whatever needed doing. On the inside, he was a butcher waiting for an excuse.

When I was a kid, maybe eight, I helped at a food stand my parents ran on weekends. Stew, mostly. Cheap, filling, always enough meat no matter how bad the times were. People lined up for it. Said it tasted better than anything they could afford anywhere else.

I didn't ask what kind of meat it was. I thought it was just… meat. Cow, pig, whatever my father had hunted.

At first, my job was small. Carrying the sacks from the shed freezer to the house. I remember the weight. The way the cold bit into my fingers through the canvas. The way my father would say, 'Don't drop that. That's good eating.'

Our shed was out back. Wooden, nothing special from the outside. Inside it was different. Hooks on the ceiling. Drain on the floor. Big chest freezer humming in the corner. Once I saw my father sharpening knives there, slow and patient, like a priest preparing for mass.

I knew something was wrong before I knew what it was. The sounds at night. The metallic smell wasn't quite like pig or cow. The way my father came in some mornings with blood up his sleeves and a light in his eyes that scared me."

He paused, swallowing hard, and for a heartbeat he looked like a boy again.

"One night," he went on, "I woke up screaming. Not loud—like somebody had a hand over their mouth. I followed the sound to the shed. Climbed up on a crate and peeked through the window.

My father had a man hanging upside down from hooks in the ceiling. Rope wrapped around his ankles. The man was still alive. His face was red, then white, then something in between.

My father was cutting into him like he was skinning a deer. The man tried to struggle, but he was tied tight. He choked on his own blood. My father stabbed him in the neck to 'drain him properly.' Steam rose in the cold air as the blood hit the floor.

I didn't move. I didn't scream. I just watched.

The next morning, my father woke me up like nothing had happened and told me to 'go clean the shed.'

That's when I saw the pieces. Little scraps of skin, hair, bits of bone caught in the cracks of the floor. I swept it all toward the drain. Then I opened the freezer.

Everything was in game bags. White. Neat. Labelled. I opened one. It was just meat. Chunks. No faces. No names.

At lunch, my mother called us in. Stew again. My favorite. I sat down, looked at the bowl, and saw that man in the shed instead of the meat. I ran outside and threw up.

It took three days before I could eat again. After that… something changed. The switch flipped. I ate greedily. I asked for more. The revulsion turned into hunger. The stew tasted better than anything I'd ever had."

He stared at the condensation on his malt.

"One morning," he said, "I walked into the shed while my father was cutting up another body. He looked at me, surprised, like I'd caught him naked. I didn't say anything. I just walked over, put on an apron, and started helping.

That was the day I joined the family business.

My first jobs were simple: undress the bodies. Wash them. Help hold them when my father made the first cuts. Then he taught me how to separate muscle from bone. How to gut without spilling anything. How to save the organs. How to cut bones small enough for broth. The heads, hands, and feet he buried. But not before taking out the brains and eyes.

My father told me he only hunted Black men. Said their meat was 'sweeter.' Said nobody would miss them like they would miss others. That's what he told himself to sleep at night.

For me, back then, it wasn't about race or any of that. It was just… normal. It was how we ate. How we lived.

We'd go out at night together. Father and son. He called it 'hunting.' We'd ride the horses or take the truck to nearby towns. Find a man walking alone, or drunk, or sleeping rough. Sometimes I was the one who pointed him out.

It felt like bonding. Like other kids, they must've felt like fishing with their dads. Only the fish walked on two legs and talked.

Once, in town, a man almost got away. A woman saw us grab him and screamed. My father panicked, dropped the man and ran. At home, he beat me for not warning him sooner.

That night, I ran too. Slept on the side of a cold road with horse manure and rats for company. I remember lying there and thinking, This is what the animals must feel like when they see us coming.

A year later, America went to war.

I thought maybe the war would take me far enough away from all of it that I could be someone else."

Vietnam, the Jungle, and the Woman With No Name

"It was 1954 when I first thought about leaving," David told me. "By then I was eating out of trash cans on bad days and helping my father butcher others. I was twenty-two when I saw the recruitment posters."

He gave a short, dry laugh.

"They said 'Be a hero. See the world.' I just wanted to get out of my house.

"I joined the Air Force. Figured if I stayed on the ground, I'd still be too close to what I knew. So I went up instead.

"By the time I was in, Vietnam was heating up. They sent me over in the mid-sixties. I worked maintenance at first—fixing planes, checking systems—but it wasn't long before I was up there on missions. I was on crews that took part in bombing runs and herbicide spraying. They called it Rolling Thunder. Operation Ranch Hand. Names that sounded clean on paper and smelled like poison in the air."

He picked at a crack in the table with a yellowed nail.

"We flew over a jungle that looked endless. Green and alive from the sky, but we were up there killing it, strip by strip. Agent Orange is raining down like strange, invisible weather. We didn't know—or we pretended we didn't know—what it would do to people on the ground. Or to us.

Then one day, they hit us back.

Anti-aircraft fire. I remember flashes below, then a sound like the world ripping. The plane shuddered. Left wing, then right. Smoke poured in. The alarms were screaming but all I heard was my own heartbeat.

We went down.

I don't remember ejecting. I remember falling. Trees rushing up. The world became green and black and pain.

I landed in a tree. Ribs broken. Breath coming in knives. It was near dark and I knew enough to know the jungle would be worse at night, so I crawled. No compass. No food. No idea where my people were or if they were even alive.

The first night, I didn't sleep. Every sound was an enemy. Insects, branches, distant voices I couldn't understand. Mosquitoes ate me alive. My broken ribs felt like they were cutting into my lungs every time I moved.

I spent three days like that. Walking, resting, walking. Drinking from leaves and muddy puddles. No food, just hunger and the echo of my grandfather's stories about winter in the mountains.

On the fourth day, it started raining and never seemed to stop. The jungle floor became mud. My boots filled with water. My feet turned white and soft and bloody. I built a little shelter out of branches, more like a pile over my head than a house, but it kept the worst of the rain off.

I tried to make traps—little pits, spring snares, sharpened stakes at the bottoms of holes. I caught one rat, maybe two. I ate them half raw because I couldn't risk making much smoke. I remember thinking about my father's shed. About how much easier it had been when someone else brought the meat."

His eyes had gone far away. Even sitting in a warm restaurant, I could almost see him still braced against jungle trees, soaked and shivering.

"I took off my boots one day to rest my feet," he said. "Skin came off with the socks in places. I put them aside to dry and must've passed out.

I woke up with a rifle butt in my mouth.

Three kids—teenagers, maybe fifteen at most—were standing around me in uniforms that looked too big for them. They were yelling in Vietnamese, pointing rifles at my chest. One tied my hands with a rope and dragged me to my feet. We walked. I was barefoot. Every step felt like fire.

They pulled me along maybe thirty steps. I stumbled and fell. The one in front yanked the rope harder. The two behind raised their rifles, shouting at me to get up. When they moved toward me, both fell into one of the pits I'd dug earlier—a hole lined with sharpened stakes.

The boy holding the rope froze. Then he bolted.

I grabbed one of the fallen rifles, aimed at his back, and shot.

The rest… that's where people stop believing me," he said, looking at me steadily. "Maybe you won't either. But you asked for everything."

His voice dropped.

"I hadn't eaten properly in over a week. My father had shown me what hunger could do. The jungle showed me the rest.

I dragged that boy's body back to my camp. I didn't build a fire—too risky. I used his own knife, made cuts the way my father taught me. Took what I could carry. Ate what I could stomach.

You can write 'allegedly' if it makes you feel better," he added with a bitter half-smile. "But for me, it was real enough."

He looked at the table, eyes glazed with memory.

"After that, I moved. The shot would bring company. I walked north, or what I thought was north. Two more days. Fever hit. My body shook. I climbed a tree and stayed up there for maybe four days—time went strange. I ate a snake that got too close. Drank rainwater off leaves.

One day, I heard voices.

Women's voices.

Four of them, walking with an ox. I climbed down, pointed a rifle, and collapsed before I could say or do anything.

When I woke up, I was on the back of that ox, covered with sacks. Someone had pressed herbs onto my ribs. My head was floating. I thought I was dead at first. Then the pain convinced me I wasn't.

The oldest woman took me in. Little stilt house away from everything, surrounded by jungle and fields. We didn't share a language. We shared work.

She fed me rice. Gave me a mat in the corner. Tended my bruises, my ribs, my fever. She hid me when soldiers from either side passed through the area. She never asked who I'd been with or what I'd done. Maybe she knew. Maybe she didn't care. The war had already taken too much from everyone.

I helped how I could. Cut wood. Repaired the hut. Hauled water. We didn't talk much, but we liked each other. Or at least, we worked well together.

When I was strong enough again, I started hunting in the jungle near her house. At first it was just animals—whatever I could catch. Sometimes we went days with only rice and roots. I'd seen hunger before. I knew the look it puts in people's eyes.

Then, one day, I came across a boy. Maybe fifteen. He'd been mauled by something—tiger, bear, I don't know. He was still breathing, holding his neck, blood coming through his fingers. He looked at me once, then he was gone.

I wasn't thinking like a soldier anymore. I was thinking like my grandfather in the snow. Like my father in the shed.

I buried what I didn't take and brought the rest home.

The old woman didn't ask questions. She just cooked. Ate. Smiled for the first time in days.

After that... boys went missing sometimes. Some stepped on old booby traps in the jungle. Some never came back from gathering wood. Vietnam was full of ghosts already. My sins blended into the war's.

I'm not telling you this to shock you," he added quietly. "I'm telling you because you wanted to know how a man gets from California to a hospital bed in Colorado with a file like mine. There are steps. There is always a path."

He took a shaky breath.

"When the war finally ended and things shifted, I woke up one morning and the old woman was gone. She'd died in her sleep. No fuss. No drama. Just gone.

I buried her behind the house. Marked it with stones. Then I realized there was nothing left for me there. No language. No place. No more excuses.

So I went home."

Coming Home, Drifting East

"Home wasn't home anymore," David continued. "California felt smaller. Dirtier. My mother was older, my father gone. He'd died while I was away. I never saw his body laid out. Never saw his hands still. Part of me thinks he just dissolved into that shed."

David said he tried to change. Got odd jobs. I tried to "be normal." Went to church where his father had once met his mother. It was there, he claimed, that he met a woman named Mary—young, kind, the sort of person who believed everyone deserved a second chance even when they hadn't earned a first.

"We fell in love fast," he said. "Too fast. I moved near my mother to 'take care of her' and hunted at night when I said I was working. We had three kids. I wanted to give them a better life than mine. But you don't build a clean house on a rotten foundation.

I stopped hunting for a while. I tried to stop drinking too. But the nightmares didn't let me sleep. Jungle, snow, sheds, kids' faces, bodies I'd cut up, things I'd done and things I'd watched.

I drank to quiet them. Drinking made everything worse.

Money got tight. Bills piled up. I got mean. Mary left. Took the kids.

One day, I kissed my mother on the forehead and told her I was going to look for work out east. I drove through Nevada, Utah, and ended up in Colorado. Pueblo. Small town. Different sky. Same demons.

I did odd jobs. Cleaning stables, hauling feed, shoveling manure. The man who hired me had a little girl. Eight years old. She ran around the yard, laughing, not afraid of anything. I looked at her and the old thoughts came back like they'd never left.

You know the rest from the court papers," he said, voice flattening. "I won't go into details anymore. I went too far. Got hit in the back of the head with a shovel before I could do what I wanted to do. Woke up in cuffs.

That was my last offense. No more hiding. No more 'suspected.' It was all on the record after that.

They put me away for life. No parole.

Old as I was getting, they knew I'd die in a cage or a ward.

Eventually, the tumor, the age, and the fact that I kept getting hurt by other inmates got me transferred here. To this place. To this bed. To you."

He looked at me. The air in the Denny's felt thin.

"You asked why," he said. "That's why. A hungry grandfather in the snow. A father who thought love was teaching his son to cut. A war that chewed people up and spat them out. A brain that never learned how to be anything but hungry and angry and empty.

Doesn't mean I'm innocent. I'm not. I'm guilty of more than they know.

But I wasn't born a monster. I was made. And when I realized it, it was already too late."

Archives, Prison, and My Own Diagnosis

After nights like that, I couldn't just go home, watch TV, and forget what I'd heard.

Instead, I went to the facility's records room.

Metal shelves. Dust. Paper boxes with names and numbers. A century's worth of people the system didn't know what else to do with.

I asked for access to the old ledgers. Read about my three residents and then kept going. Files from the 1920s, 1950s, 1980s. Men and women with diagnoses: schizophrenia, bipolar disorder, severe depression, psychosis, personality disorders, brain injuries. The crimes ranged from theft and arson to murder and things worse than murder.

Some were like David—long histories of violence and trauma. Others were people who'd had one break, one bad night, one unmedicated psychotic episode that changed everything. Many had childhoods that read like horror stories: beatings, neglect, incest, hunger, parents in prison or gone.

Sitting there under the buzzing fluorescent lights, I realized something I didn't want to see:

I had been chasing chaos my whole life too.

I'd had dozens of jobs, side hustles, criminal schemes, attempts at reinvention. Construction, side businesses, selling drugs, working in corrections, then as a coroner's transport, then back to hospitals, then into this mental health facility. Always moving. Always searching. Always restless.

I wasn't a serial killer. I wasn't a child molester. I hadn't done what David had done. But I recognized the pattern of never being able to sit with myself. The need for adrenaline. The sabotage. The depression. The rush of starting something new and the crash when it fell apart.

Later, after my own run-ins with the law, after another night in a cell staring at concrete and listening to other men snore, I finally heard the question they always ask in prison:

"What are you in for?"

I said my charge: DUI.

Some were there for : attempted murder, armed robbery, dealing, assaults, things they weren't proud of but wore like armor, and way too many claimed innocence. Many were on meds. Bipolar. Schizophrenic. Traumatized. Sleep-deprived. Lost.

That's when it hit me:

We like to think prisons and mental wards are full of evil people.

Most of them are sick people.

Not innocent. Not harmless. But I'm sick. Untreated. Unmedicated. Unheard.

Modern criminology supports this. Studies from the National Institute of Mental Health show that more than 64% of incarcerated men have a diagnosable mental disorder. Trauma alters the brain's amygdala, hippocampus, and prefrontal cortex — the very systems responsible for fear, judgment, and impulse control. Neuroscientists found that children exposed to chronic violence develop "survival wiring" instead of "trust wiring," a pattern nearly identical to soldiers returning from combat.

The DSM-5 notes that severe childhood trauma can mimic or worsen disorders like bipolar, ADHD, and borderline personality disorder — creating emotional volatility that looks like defiance or criminality, but is rooted in neurological injury.

I started therapy at thirty-three. Sat down and agreed to do what I'd asked David to do: go back to the beginning and ask why.

I learned words I wish I'd heard earlier:

- ADHD — Attention Deficit Hyperactivity Disorder

- Bipolar Disorder

- Depression

I realized all the restless jobs, the side hustles, the criminal risks, the love for chaos, the inability to stay steady — they weren't just character flaws. They were symptoms.

According to behavioral genetics research from the University of Virginia, untreated ADHD increases the likelihood of addiction, criminal impulsivity, and "high-stimulation seeking," because the brain is constantly craving dopamine regulation. Bipolar disorder intensifies this further — manic phases create risk-taking, grandiosity, sleeplessness, and irrational confidence. Depression creates numbness that people try to escape any way they can.

It didn't excuse anything I'd done. But it explained it.

Just like trauma and sickness explained parts of David's life without erasing his responsibility.

Monsters are not born in cribs.

They are built in sheds, in war zones, in homes where love is twisted and hunger becomes normal.

They are shaped by brains that never develop right and by societies that punish symptoms instead of treating causes.

And science backs it:

The ACE Study (Adverse Childhood Experiences) found that kids exposed to severe trauma are 4,000% more likely to develop destructive coping behaviors.

4,000%.

When the brain is raised in survival mode, it creates a psychological "inner creature" — what Jung called the Shadow, what neuroscientists call the defensive self, and what men like us call the demons.

Every human has them.

Some learn to control them through support, therapy, or a stable home.

Others never get the chance.

And some are forced to become that monster — because the alternative is to be eaten alive by their environment. In violent neighborhoods, cartels, poverty, and abuse, becoming the monster isn't a choice; it's self-defense. Not morally right — but psychologically predictable.

Researchers call this adaptive antisocial behavior:

when the environment is so dangerous that aggression becomes survival.

Monsters are not myths.

They are trauma wearing a human face.

And the difference between the ones who control their demons and the ones controlled by them often comes down to one word:

Help.

EPILOGUE

The Vampire's Shadow

David died a few months after that September appointment. Complications from the tumor, from age, from years of institutional food and weight carried too long. On paper, his death was ordinary:

Cause of death: natural causes.

Nothing about his chart said vampire or monster or boy who watched his father cut men up in a shed.

No visitors came for his body. No pastor said his name out loud at a funeral. No one lit a candle for him on purpose.

But his story stayed with me.

The winter in the mountains.
 The shed.
 The war.
 The old woman in the jungle who gave him shelter without knowing what he really was.
 The little girl in Pueblo whose life intersected with his at the worst possible moment.
 The patients in the facility whose crimes were smaller but whose pain was just as deep.
 And my own reflection in the glass, wondering what kind of monster I might've become if my path had been just a little different.

History is full of tragedies like his, even without the cannibalism.

Families displaced by war. Children molded by violence. Veterans brought home but never brought back. People punished for acting out symptoms nobody taught them to recognize.

Modern psychology gives us better language now. We can talk about trauma, attachment disorders, brain changes from chronic stress. We can diagnose. We can medicate. We can treat.

But it all comes too late for some.

David once told me he wished he'd had a different beginning.

I can't give that to him.

What I can do is what I'm doing here:

Write it down.
 Tell the story.
 Not to glorify him.
 Not to excuse him.

But to warn us.

Because as long as we keep pretending monsters are born out of nowhere, we'll keep making new ones in the dark.

www.ingramcontent.com/pod-product-compliance
Lightning Source LLC
Chambersburg PA
CBHW031447270326
41930CB00007B/905